AU+IBD

V

THE STATES AND THEIR SYMBOLS

Washington, D.C.
Facts and Symbols

by Kathy Feeney

Consultant:
Donna C. Desormeaux
Media Relations Manager
Washington, D.C., Convention and Visitors Association

Hilltop Books

an imprint of Capstone Press
Mankato, Minnesota

Hilltop Books are published by Capstone Press
151 Good Counsel Drive, P.O. Box 669, Mankato, Minnesota 56002
http://www.capstone-press.com

Library of Congress Cataloging-in-Publication Data
Feeney, Kathy, 1954–
    Washington, D.C. facts and symbols/by Kathy Feeney.
    p. cm.—(The states and their symbols)
    Includes bibliographical references (p. 23) and index.
    Summary: Presents information about Washington, D.C., its nickname, motto,
and emblems.
    ISBN 0-7368-0527-3
    1. Emblems, State—Washington (D.C.)—Juvenile literature. [1. Emblems,
State—Washington (D.C.) 2. Washington (D.C.)] I. Title. II. Series.
CR203.W3.F44 2000
975.3—dc21   99-053460

Editorial Credits
Karen L. Daas, editor; Linda Clavel, production designer and illustrator;
    Kimberly Danger, photo researcher

Photo Credits
C. J. Pickerell/FPG International LLC, 20
One Mile Up, Inc., 8, 10 (inset)
Photo Agora, 6, 10
Rob and Ann Simpson, 14
Root Resources/MacDonald Photography, 22 (bottom)
Unicorn Stock Photos/Dick Keen, cover; Phyllis Kedl, 16; Martha McBride, 18;
    Florent Flipper, 22 (middle)
Visuals Unlimited/Vidakovic, 12; Jeffrey Howe, 22 (top)

1 2 3 4 5 6 05 04 03 02 01 00

Table of Contents

Map 4
Fast Facts 5
The Nation's Capital 7
The District and Its Flag 9
Name and Nickname 11
Seal and Motto 13
District Bird 15
District Tree 17
District Flower 19
The National Mall 21

Places to Visit 22
Words to Know 23
Read More 23
Useful Addresses 24
Internet Sites 24
Index 24

Maryland

WASHINGTON, D.C.

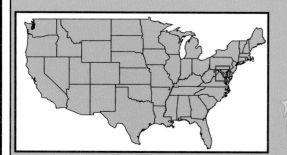

Georgetown

The White House   Ford's Theatre National Historic Site

The National Mall

Virginia

Anacostia River

Potomac River

Capital: Washington, D.C., is the capital of the United States of America.

Size: Washington, D.C., covers 68 square miles (176 square kilometers).

Location: Washington, D.C., is in the eastern United States. Virginia and Maryland border the district.

Population: 523,124 people live in Washington, D.C. (U.S. Census Bureau, 1998 estimate).

Founding Date: President George Washington declared Washington, D.C., the nation's capital in 1791.

Major Industries: The offices of the U.S. federal government are based in Washington, D.C. The city is popular with travelers around the world. Nearly 20 million people visit Washington, D.C., each year.

The Nation's Capital

Washington, D.C., is the capital of the United States. D.C. stands for "District of Columbia." A district is a small area. Washington, D.C., is not part of any state.

Washington, D.C., is the center of the nation's government. The president of the United States lives and works in Washington, D.C. Members of the U.S. Congress meet there. Representatives and senators from each state make up Congress. Congress meets in the U.S. Capitol to make laws.

Members of the Supreme Court also meet in Washington, D.C. Supreme Court justices judge cases that relate to the U.S. Constitution.

The nation's capital is home to several monuments. These monuments honor U.S. soldiers and past U.S. presidents. The Vietnam Veterans Memorial, the Jefferson Memorial, and the Washington Monument are in Washington, D.C.

The Jefferson Memorial is near the Potomac River. This memorial honors President Thomas Jefferson.

The District and Its Flag

Washington, D.C., is the only place in the United States that does not belong to a state. The country's founders did not want the nation's capital to be part of a state. They feared a state with the nation's capital might have more power than other states.

In 1791, George Washington chose the location for the capital. He chose an area along the Potomac River. The land he chose belonged to Maryland and Virginia. Both states agreed to give their land for the capital.

Washington selected Pierre L'Enfant to design the capital. L'Enfant's plan included wide tree-lined streets, large public parks, grand buildings, and a long, grassy mall.

Washington, D.C., adopted its flag in 1938. The flag has a white background. Three red stars appear above two horizontal red stripes. The flag looks like the Washington family's coat of arms.

The Potomac River borders Washington, D.C.

Washington, D.C., is named for George Washington. He was the first president of the United States. He also selected the land for the nation's capital.

Before Washington, D.C., the United States did not have a permanent capital. Philadelphia, Pennsylvania; Princeton, New Jersey; and New York, New York, once were national capitals. Washington planned to name the permanent capital Federal City. But government officials named the capital Washington, D.C.

D.C. stands for District of Columbia. "Columbia" honors Italian explorer Christopher Columbus. He sailed to North America from Spain in 1492.

Washington, D.C., has three nicknames. It is called the Nation's Capital, the Capital City, and America's First City because it is the capital of the United States.

The Capitol is one of many U.S. government buildings in Washington, D.C.

Washington, D.C., adopted its official seal in 1871. The seal represents the district's government. The seal also makes government papers official.

The Washington, D.C., seal has two figures in the center. George Washington rests his hand on an ax. The ax stands for power. A woman wearing a blindfold holds a wreath and a tablet. She represents justice.

Several features of the district appear on the seal. The Potomac River appears in the background. The Potomac River borders Washington, D.C. The U.S. Capitol and a train also are in the background. They represent the government and the growth of Washington, D.C.

The Washington, D.C., motto is "Justitia Omnibus." This Latin phrase means "Justice for All." The motto appears on a ribbon at the bottom of the district seal.

A woman on the Washington, D.C., seal holds a tablet that says, "Constitution." The Constitution is a written document that contains the laws of the U.S. government.

District Bird

The wood thrush became Washington, D.C.'s, official bird in 1967. Wood thrushes are songbirds.

Adult wood thrushes grow to about 8 inches (20 centimeters) long. They have a brown upper body and a red head. Their sides and lower body are white with large spots. Wood thrushes have a brown bill.

Wood thrushes live in wooded areas. Some wood thrushes live near farms and gardens. Farmers and gardeners like wood thrushes because they eat beetles and caterpillars that sometimes attack crops. Wood thrushes also eat berries.

Wood thrushes build their nests with leaves, grass, and mud. They hide their cup-shaped nests in thick bushes. Female wood thrushes lay three or four eggs twice each year. Their eggs are blue or green. Young wood thrushes leave their nests 12 to 13 days after hatching.

Wood thrushes blend with their surroundings. People are more likely to hear wood thrushes than to see them.

District Tree

Washington, D.C., officials chose the scarlet oak as the district tree in 1960. Scarlet oaks grow naturally in sandy and rocky areas. People also plant scarlet oaks in parks and yards throughout the capital.

The scarlet oak tree gets its name from its leaves. Its green leaves turn bright red in the fall.

Scarlet oaks have light brown, oval-shaped acorns. A white kernel is inside these acorns. Many animals eat these kernels. Squirrels and birds eat scarlet oak acorn kernels.

The bark of a young scarlet oak is light brown. The bark is very smooth. The bark becomes rough and turns dark red as the scarlet oak ages.

Scarlet oaks belong to the red oak family. Scarlet oaks also are called Spanish oaks and red oaks.

Scarlet oaks grow 60 to 80 feet (18 to 24 meters) tall.

District Flower

The Washington, D.C., district flower is the American Beauty rose. District officials adopted the flower in 1925.

The American Beauty rose is famous for its appearance. The flower has deep pink petals and oval-shaped leaves. The rose's long, green stem is covered with thorns. Many people recognize American Beauty roses by their pleasant scent.

A botanist created the American Beauty rose. These scientists study flowers and plants. Botanists sometimes develop new varieties of flowers from two separate varieties.

People do not know where the American Beauty rose was first grown. Some people believe the flower was brought to the United States from France. Other people believe the American Beauty rose was first grown in the White House garden.

American Beauty roses can grow to be 6 feet (2 meters) tall.

The National Mall

The National Mall is a large park that runs from the U.S. Capitol to the Potomac River. Many of the nation's most important buildings are on the Mall.

The Mall covers 146 acres (59 hectares). The U.S. Capitol stands at the eastern end of the Mall. This area is called Capitol Hill. The Washington Monument is at the halfway point on the Mall. This monument honors President George Washington. The Lincoln Memorial is at the western end of the Mall. This large statue honors President Abraham Lincoln.

The Smithsonian Institution is along the Mall. The Smithsonian Institution is the world's largest museum. It is made up of 16 museums. The National Air and Space Museum, the National Zoological Park, and the National Museum of Natural History are part of the Smithsonian Institution.

The eastern half of the National Mall stretches from Capitol Hill (right) to the Washington Monument (left). The Washington Monument is the tallest building in the district.

Places to Visit

Ford's Theatre National Historic Site

President Abraham Lincoln was shot at Ford's Theatre. John Wilkes Booth shot the president during a performance of *Our American Cousin*. Visitors tour the theater, the Lincoln Museum, and the Peterson House. Visitors also watch a live theater performance.

Georgetown

Georgetown offers a mix of American history and modern attractions. Visitors shop at Georgetown Park or view thousands of artifacts at the Georgetown Park Museum. Visitors also take a walking tour of buildings from the 1700s. Several historic homes are included in this tour.

The White House

The president and the president's family live in the White House. Every U.S. president has lived in this 132-room mansion except George Washington. But Washington chose the building's location. Visitors tour seven rooms, including the library and State Dining Room.

Words to Know

artifact (ART-uh-fakt)—an object made or used by human beings in the past

botanist (BOT-uh-nist)—a scientist who studies flowers and plants

coat of arms (KOHT UHV ARMS)—a design that stands for a family, city, state, or organization

Constitution (kon-stuh-TOO-shun)—the written document containing the laws by which the United States is governed

explorer (ex-SPLOR-ur)—a person who travels to a new place to discover what it is like

mall (MAWL)—a long, grassy area; many monuments and memorials are on the National Mall.

Read More

Elish, Dan. *Washington, D.C.* Celebrate the States. New York: Benchmark Books, 1998.

Kummer, Patricia K. *Washington, D.C.* One Nation. Mankato, Minn.: Capstone Books, 1998.

Stein, R. Conrad. *Washington, D.C.* America the Beautiful. New York: Children's Press, 1999.

Thompson, Kathleen. *Washington, D.C.* Portrait of America. Austin, Texas: Raintree Steck-Vaughn, 1996.

Useful Addresses

Washington, D.C., Chamber of Commerce
1301 Pennsylvania Avenue NW
Washington, DC 20004

Washington, D.C., Convention and Visitors Association
1212 New York Avenue NW
Suite 600
Washington, DC 20005-3992

Internet Sites

Stately Knowledge: Washington, D.C.
http://www.ipl.org/youth/stateknow/dc1.html
Washington, D.C., Convention and Visitors Association
http://www.washington.org
Washington, D.C., Facts & Information
http://www.pe.net/~rksnow/dc.htm

Index

American Beauty rose, 19
Columbus, Christopher, 11
Congress, 7
Jefferson Memorial, 7
L'Enfant, Pierre, 9
Lincoln Memorial, 21
Potomac River, 9, 13, 21
scarlet oak tree, 17
Smithsonian Institution, 21
Supreme Court, 7
U.S. Capitol, 7, 13, 21
Washington, George, 9, 11, 13, 21
Washington Monument, 7, 21
wood thrush, 15